Let's Get Mapping!

How to Read a Map

Melanie Waldron

Chicago, Illinois

To contact Capstone Global Library please
phone 800-747-4992, or visit our web site
www.capstonepub.com

Edited by Nancy Dickmann and Abby Colich
Designed by Victoria Allen
Original illustrations © 2013
Illustrated by HL Studios
Picture research by Ruth Blair
Originated by Capstone Global Library Limited
Printed and bound in China by CTPS

17 16 15 14 13 12
10 9 8 7 6 5 4 3 2 1

**Library of Congress Cataloging-in-Publication
Data**
Waldron, Melanie.
How to read a map / Melanie Waldron.
p. cm.—(Let's get mapping!)
Includes bibliographical references and index.
ISBN 978-1-4109-4899-1 (hb)—ISBN 978-1-4109-
4906-6 (pb)
1. Map reading. I. Title.
GA151.W26 2013
912.01'4—dc23   2012008416

Acknowledgments

We would like to thank the following for
permission to reproduce photographs: Alamy:
pp. 7 (© avatra images), 9 (© The Art Gallery
Collection), 11 (© Rob Walls), 13 (© Jim Wileman),
21 (© Radius Images); Corbis: pp. 23 (© Ocean),
27 (© Ashley Jouhar/cultura); © Lovell Johns
Ltd 2012: pp. 16; Shutterstock: pp. 4 (© zhu
difeng), 5 (© Anton Gvozdikov), 12 (© Mark
Yuill), 17 (© upthebanner), 24 (© Peteri), 26 (©
Stocksnapper).

Cover photograph of boy reading a city map
at a resort reproduced with permission from
Superstock (© Corbis).

Background and design features reproduced
with permission from Shutterstock.

Every effort has been made to contact
copyright holders of any material reproduced
in this book. Any omissions will be rectified
in subsequent printings if notice is given to
the publisher.

Contents

Some words appear in the text in bold, **like this**. You can find out what they mean by looking in the glossary.

Marvelous Maps

Most maps are flat drawings of the land. They show the land from a "bird's-eye view." This means that they show what it looks like from above. Maps are full of information. They can tell you things about Earth's **natural features**. They can also tell you about the things that humans have built on the land, such as roads and buildings. Maps can even give you information about things that you cannot see. For example, a map can show how much money people earn in different countries.

Maps can show a bird's-eye view of roads like these.

How are maps used?

People use maps to help them travel around. We can also use them to find places and to learn about places and the people living there. Maps can also be used to show how the land has changed over time.

People use maps to help them find their way around.

OLD MAPS, NEW MAPS

People have been making maps for hundreds of years. Many older maps were made by explorers using sketches of the areas they explored. Today, most maps are made with the help of **satellite images** and **aerial photographs**.

A World of Maps

Different types of maps can show very different things about the same area of land. A map of your country might show the towns and cities as well as the **borders** between regions or states. A different map might show how the land is used—for example, for farming or forestry. Some maps can give very detailed information about the buildings in an area.

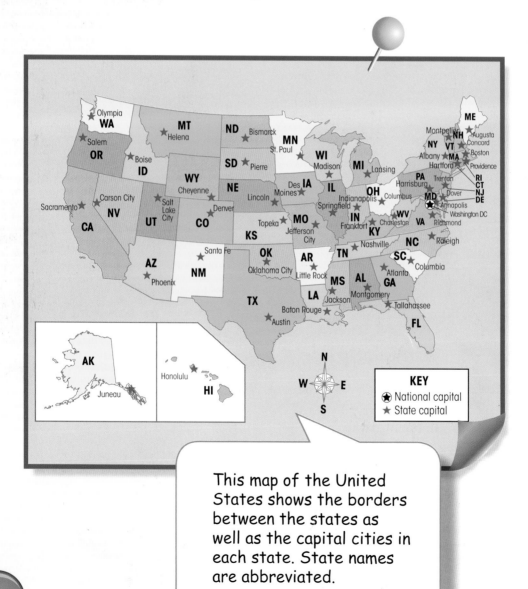

This map of the United States shows the borders between the states as well as the capital cities in each state. State names are abbreviated.

Travel maps

Many maps are designed to help people travel from place to place. Road maps show all the roads in an area, as well as the towns and cities they connect. Railroad maps show different railroad lines and the stations that link them together. Some maps show air travel routes across the world.

Maps of central areas are often displayed in public places. They can help people find their way around a town or city.

PAPER OR DIGITAL?

Many maps are printed onto folded sheets of paper or are bound into books. Lots of **digital maps** can be found on the Internet. Some digital maps can be downloaded from a computer onto handsets you can carry around, like cell phones.

Layers of Information

There is a lot of information about the land that a map could show. It could show buildings and what they are used for. It could show the type of **vegetation** growing on the land. A map could show the many different streams, rivers, and lakes in an area.

This map shows how land is used in the United States. You couldn't use this map to plan a train trip!

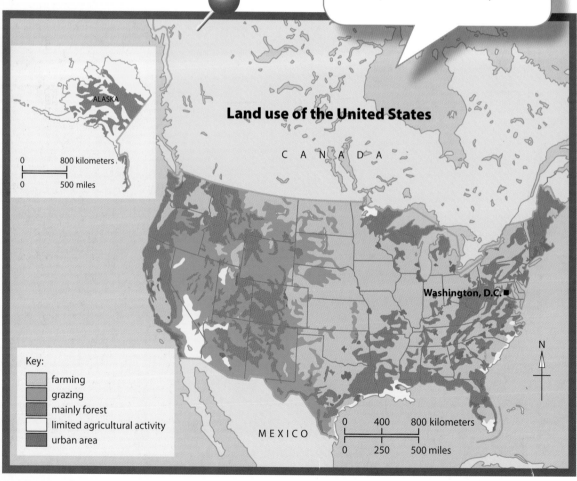

Land use of the United States

ALASKA

0 — 800 kilometers
0 — 500 miles

CANADA

Washington, D.C. ■

N

MEXICO

0   400   800 kilometers
0   250   500 miles

Key:
- farming
- grazing
- mainly forest
- limited agricultural activity
- urban area

Cartographers are people who make maps. They must select the information they need for each type of map they are making. For example, to make a map of a town that shows all the different buildings, they would not need to show the type of rock underneath the ground.

Map titles

When you look at a map, it is important to understand what the map is trying to show you. The map title is a good clue! Make sure you read the title first.

UNMAPPED LANDS

In the 1700s, many European explorers traveled west across North America. They created and used maps as they went. Many of these maps had huge blank areas. These areas showed places that had not yet been explored.

Map Symbols

Maps use symbols to represent different things. A symbol is a small dot, picture, line, or shape that is easy to spot. For example, a blue line might mean a highway, while a black line might mean a railroad line. Trees could represent an area of forest, and gray shapes could represent buildings.

If a map has a few different symbols, it should also have a **key** to explain what each symbol means. A key lists each symbol and what it represents. If a map has symbols, you should look for the key to help you understand the map.

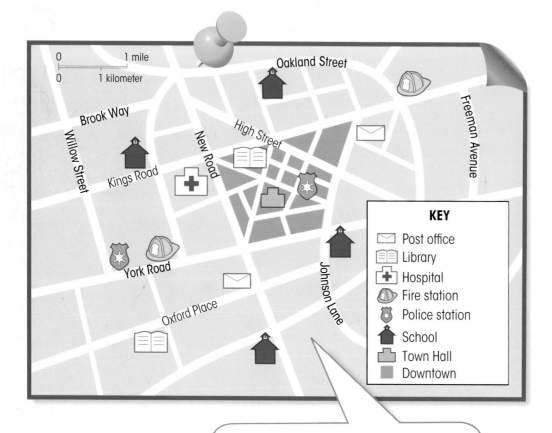

This map uses little pictures as symbols. Look at the key. Can you see why these pictures have been chosen?

PICTORIAL MAPS

It is not just symbols that can represent things on maps. Sometimes mapmakers draw tiny pictures of the actual buildings. These maps are called **pictorial maps**. They are mostly used in areas with many tourists. They are pretty to look at, and they help people to find buildings or special places of interest in a town or city.

Which Way Is Up?

If you are using a map to help you find your way around, or to find a certain place, you need to make sure the map is facing in the right direction! To help you do this, mapmakers usually print a **compass rose** on the map. This tells you which way is north, south, east, and west on the map.

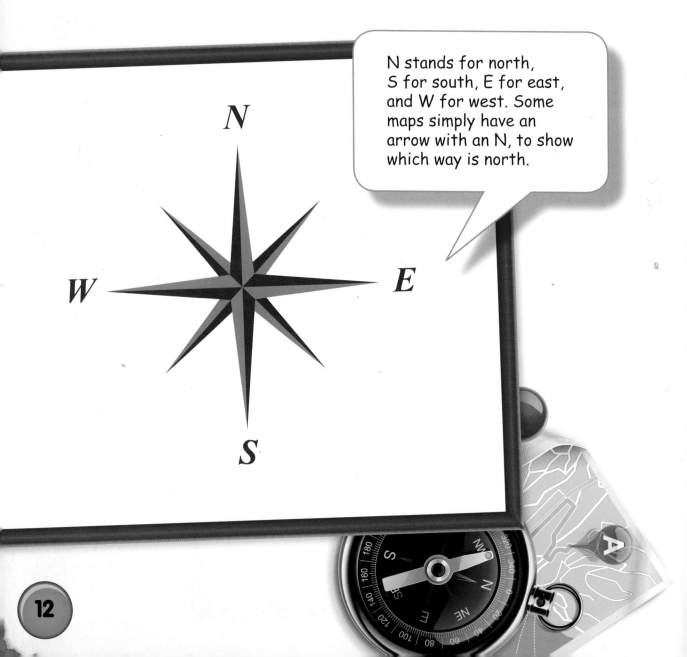

N stands for north, S for south, E for east, and W for west. Some maps simply have an arrow with an N, to show which way is north.

Finding north

The compass rose shows you where north is on the map. To make sure the map is facing the right direction, you need to find where north is on the ground. To do this, you can use a **compass**.

The red arrow on a compass always points to north. Hold the compass flat and see which direction the red arrow is pointing toward. This is north. Now you can turn the map so that north on the map is the same as north on the ground.

Using a compass and a map together is useful in the countryside, where there are no street names to help you.

Shades of Color

Sometimes maps are used to show different amounts or measurements of things. This could be the height of land above sea level or the number of people living in an area.

Mapmakers can use color to show how the amount of something changes across the land. For example, maps showing land height often show low land as green. As the land gets higher, the color changes to yellow, then orange, then brown or purple. Very high land in mountainous areas is often shown as white.

This map shows the height of the land in southern Africa. Look at the key to see where the highest land is.

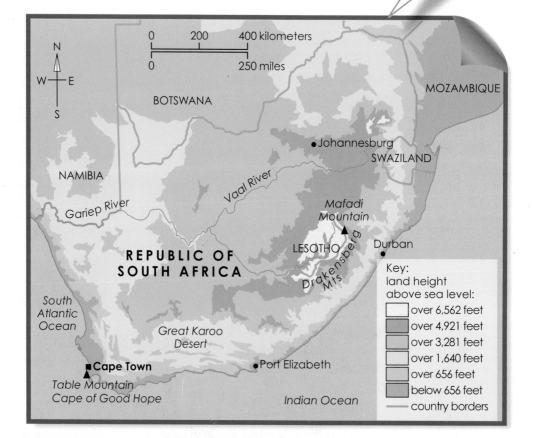

BOTSWANA

MOZAMBIQUE

• Johannesburg

SWAZILAND

NAMIBIA

Vaal River

Gariep River

Mafadi Mountain

LESOTHO

Durban

REPUBLIC OF SOUTH AFRICA

Drakensberg Mts

South Atlantic Ocean

Great Karoo Desert

• Port Elizabeth

■ Cape Town

Table Mountain
Cape of Good Hope

Indian Ocean

0   200   400 kilometers
0   250 miles

Key:
land height above sea level:
- over 6,562 feet
- over 4,921 feet
- over 3,281 feet
- over 1,640 feet
- over 656 feet
- below 656 feet
- — country borders

Similar shades

When you look at a color-shaded map, make sure you read the key first. Then you will know what each color represents. Sometimes mapmakers use shades of one color that are very similar. It can be hard to tell which color is which on the map! But using shades can help you to spot patterns on a map.

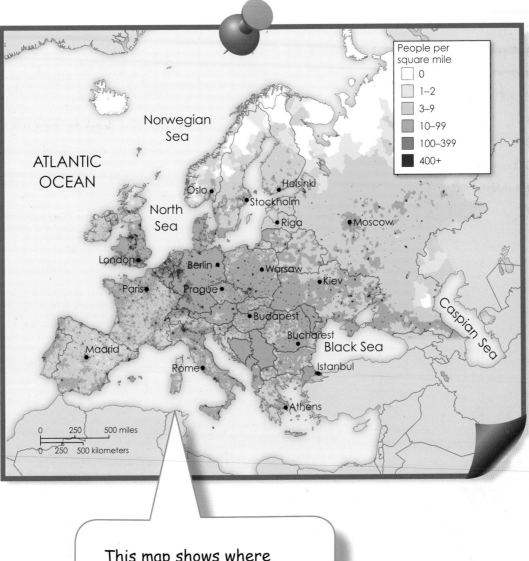

This map shows where people live in Europe. You can see that there are lots of people living around the large cities.

Contour Lines

Some maps give a lot of detailed information about the height of the land. These maps are usually of small areas, rather than whole countries or **continents**. People such as hikers and rock climbers use them.

Mapmakers use **contour lines** on maps to show the height of the land. Contour lines follow the land at the same height above sea level. For example, a 1,500-foot (457-meter) contour line would run along all the land that is 1,500 feet (457 meters) above sea level.

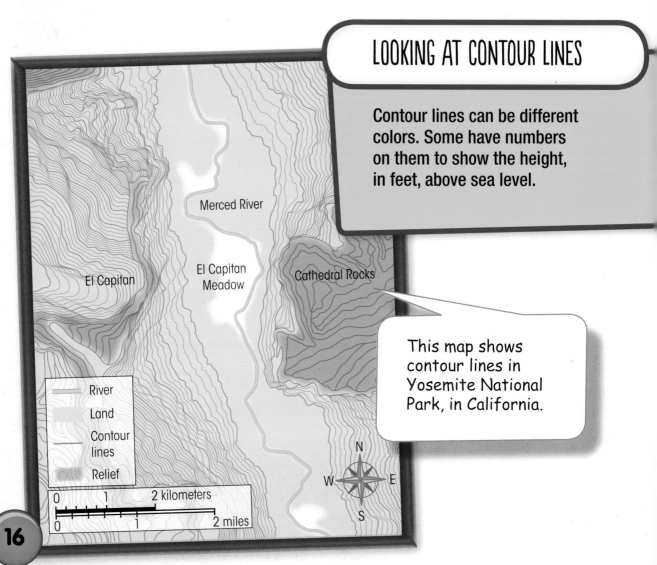

LOOKING AT CONTOUR LINES

Contour lines can be different colors. Some have numbers on them to show the height, in feet, above sea level.

Merced River

El Capitan

El Capitan Meadow

Cathedral Rocks

This map shows contour lines in Yosemite National Park, in California.

River

Land

Contour lines

Relief

0   1   2 kilometers

0   1   2 miles

N
W   E
S

Line spacing

Contour lines are spaced at intervals. For example, one line might show land that is 30 feet (9 meters) higher than the next line. Steep land is shown by contour lines packed closely together. This is because the land height rises by 30 feet in a short distance. Land that is quite flat has contour lines spaced far apart, because there is a further distance to go before the land height rises by 30 feet.

You can see the steep **valley** sides in Yosemite here.

Map Scales

Maps are always smaller than the land they show—otherwise they would be life-size! Maps are scaled-down versions of the land. This means that everything is shrunk down. Maps can be shrunk down by different amounts.

Small and large scale

Small-scale maps shrink everything down a lot. This means that a large area, like a whole country, can be shown on one map. However, there is not very much local detail on small-scale maps. Large-scale maps shrink everything down a bit less. This means that only a smaller area, such as a town, can be shown on one map. More local detail can be included on large-scale maps.

Scale ratios

Some maps have **scale ratios** written on them. A small-scale map ratio could be written 1:100,000. This means that 1 inch on the map equals 100,000 inches (about 1.5 miles, or 2.4 kilometers) in real life. This might be useful for going on a car journey. A large-scale map ratio could be written 1:24,000, where 1 inch on the map equals 24,000 inches (2,000 feet, or 610 meters) in real life. This might be useful for finding your way around a town on foot.

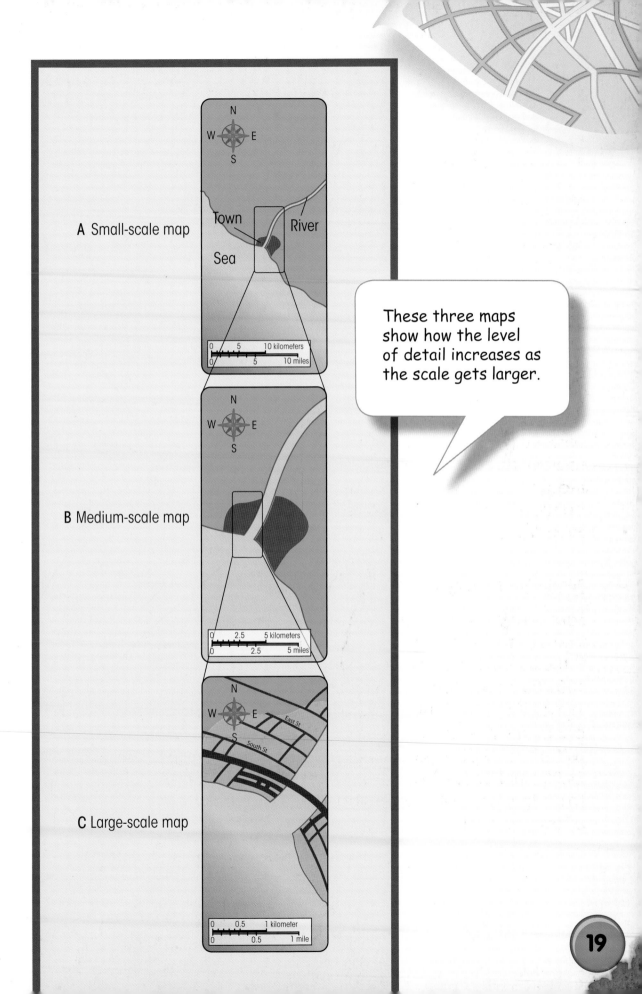

A Small-scale map

B Medium-scale map

C Large-scale map

These three maps show how the level of detail increases as the scale gets larger.

Finding the Distance

When you are using a map, it is sometimes useful to figure out a distance in real life. Many maps have a **bar scale** printed on them, to help you do this. A bar scale is a line, or a bar, that has distances marked on it. You can use a ruler to measure the distance you want to figure out on the map. You can then hold the ruler against the bar scale to see how far this is in real life.

Use the bar scale in this map to figure out the distance between the park and the school.

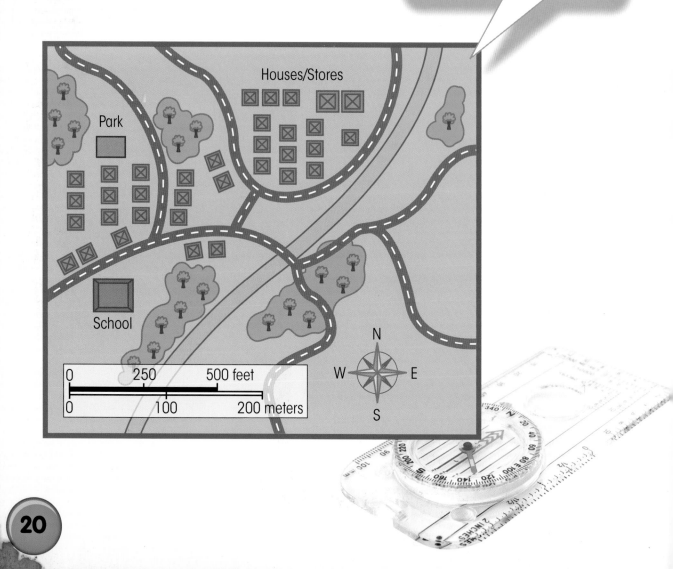

Measuring curvy lines

You can use a straight edge, such as a ruler, to measure distances between two points on a map. However, you might want to know the length of a river. Not many rivers flow in perfectly straight lines! You could use a piece of string to follow the river on the map, bending it around corners. You could then hold the string straight against the bar scale, to find out the distance.

It is useful to know how far a path might take you. You can use the scale to figure out this distance.

Lines of Latitude and Longitude

Lines of **latitude** are imaginary lines that circle around Earth. We measure lines of latitude in degrees. The **equator** is a line of latitude. It circles all the way around the middle of Earth and has a position of 0 degrees. Each line above and below the equator goes up one degree until the North and South Poles. They are 90 degrees north and south of the equator.

Longitude

Lines of **longitude** run from the top to the bottom of Earth. Each one passes through the North and South Poles. The **prime meridian** is the central line of longitude, and it has a position of 0 degrees. All the other lines are measured in degrees east or west of the prime meridian.

ORANGES AND CAKES

Lines of longitude all meet at the North and South Poles. They split Earth into wedges, like an orange. Lines of latitude never meet. They split Earth up into layers, like a round cake.

Lines of latitude run in parallel, straight lines around Earth. Lines of longitude are imaginary lines that run from the top to the bottom of Earth.

prime meridian

North Pole (90 degrees North)

equator (0 degrees)

South Pole (90 degrees South)

Pinpointing Positions

We can use lines of latitude and longitude to find a location on Earth's surface. For example, the city of Moscow, in Russia, is where latitude line 55 degrees North meets longitude line 37 degrees East.

On maps of much smaller areas, lines of latitude and longitude are a bit too far apart to be useful. Instead, maps can use grids to help locate things. Grids are made up of lines running across and lines running up and down. They make small squares on the map. Often, the bottom sides of the squares are named with letters. The left side are named with numbers.

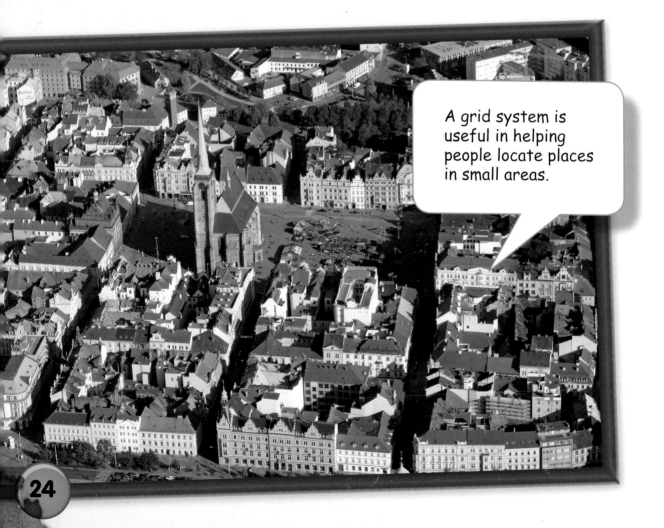

A grid system is useful in helping people locate places in small areas.

Using grid lines

All the squares on a map grid have their own **grid reference**. To find a square's grid reference, look at the letters running along the bottom of the map. Find the letter for the square. Now do the same for the numbers running up the side of the map. Put the letter and the number together, and you have a grid reference.

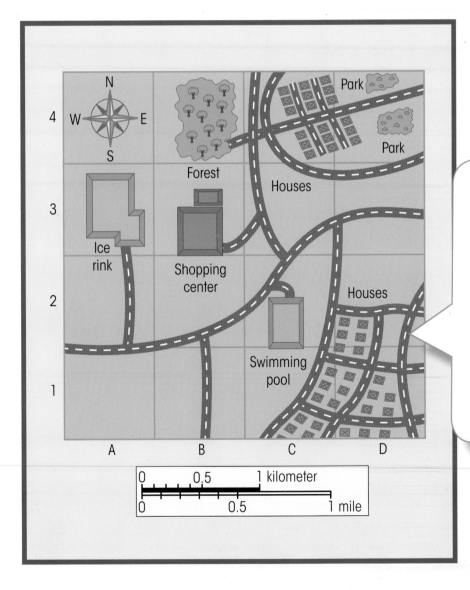

In this map, the square containing the swimming pool has a grid reference of C2. Can you find the correct grid reference for the square containing the ice rink?

Using Maps

Map reading is a really useful skill! It can help you get around and find places. But with modern technology, you don't always need to be able to read a map. Satellites can send signals to receivers such as **GPS** handsets and even cell phones. These can then use a screen to show where you are on the map. They can also direct you to where you need to go.

However, you should not always rely on this technology, as batteries can run out and gadgets can break down. Learning good map-reading skills is important, too.

GPS handsets can help you get around easily.

Remember some important steps in map reading:

- Make sure you have the correct map of the correct area.
- Make sure you know what the map is trying to show you.
- Make sure you know which direction the map should go—use the compass rose.
- Look at the map symbols and the key so you know what features to look out for.
- Look at the scale so that you can judge how far away things are.
- Look at the grid to see if that can help you find the information you need.

Get Mapping!

Look at this map. Can you use the title, key, scale, and grid to answer the following questions?

This map shows how land is used in the United States.

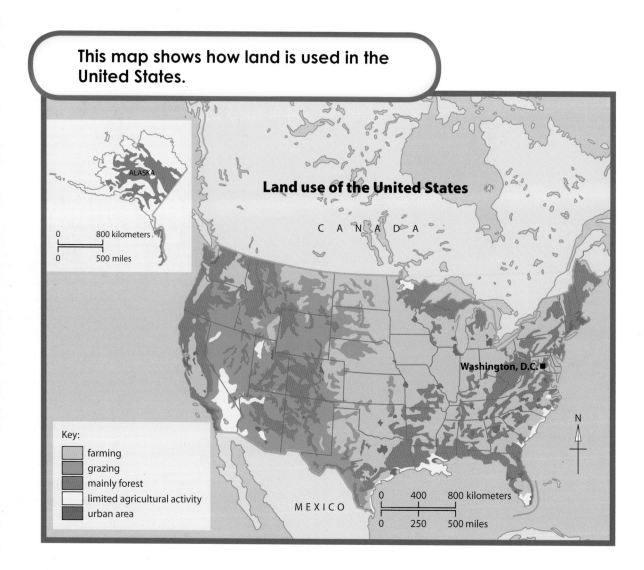

Land use of the United States

C A N A D A

ALASKA

0   800 kilometers

0   500 miles

Washington, D.C. ■

N

Key:
- farming
- grazing
- mainly forest
- limited agricultural activity
- urban area

M E X I C O

0   400   800 kilometers

0   250   500 miles

1) What is the purpose of this map?

2) What do the green areas show?

3) What do the red areas show?

4) What do the blue areas show?

5) Is Mexico to the north or south of the United States?

6) What area of the United States has the most land for farming?

7) What area of the United States has the most urban area?

8) Using the bar scale, estimate how many miles it is from Washington, D.C., to the West Coast.

Glossary

aerial photograph photograph taken from high above Earth's surface, usually from an airplane

bar scale bar or line on a map that shows us how far a distance in real life is represented on the map

border imaginary line that separates different countries or different regions inside a country

cartographer person who makes maps

compass instrument with a needle that always points north

compass rose drawing with four points, showing where north, south, east, and west are on a map

continent one of Earth's seven major areas of land: North America, South America, Europe, Africa, Asia, Australia, and Antarctica

contour line line that follows all the land at a certain height above sea level

digital map map that is shown on a screen, such as a computer or cell phone screen

equator imaginary circle around Earth that is halfway between the North and South Poles

GPS (global positioning system) system that uses signals from satellites to find your exact location and to direct you to another location

grid reference figure made up of numbers and letters, or just numbers, that allows you to pinpoint a place on a map

key list of symbols and an explanation of what each one represents

latitude distance between the equator and a point north or south on Earth's surface. The distance is measured in degrees.

longitude distance on Earth's surface that is east or west of the prime meridian. The distance is measured in degrees.

natural feature something on Earth's surface that has been created by nature—for example, a mountain

pictorial map map with tiny drawings of the features it wants to show, which is often used in tourist areas

prime meridian imaginary line on Earth's surface that goes from the North Pole to the South Pole and passes through Greenwich, England

satellite image picture, like a photograph, that a satellite can take of Earth from space

scale ratio number that tells us how far a distance in real life is represented on a map

valley long area of low land between two steep, sloping hillsides

vegetation all the plants growing on Earth's surface

Find Out More

There is a whole world of maps and mapping waiting to be discovered! Try looking at some other books and some web sites to get started.

Books

Henzel, Cynthia Kennedy. *Reading Maps* (On the Map). Edina, Minn.: ABDO, 2008.

Johnson, Jinny. *Maps and Mapping* (Inside Access). Boston: Kingfisher, 2007.

Torpie, Kate. *Reading Maps* (All Over the Map). New York: Crabtree, 2008.

Web sites

education.nationalgeographic.com/education/multimedia/ interactive/maps-tools-adventure-island/kd/?ar_a=3
Play this interactive game to learn more about how symbols on a map work.

www.nationalatlas.gov
This U.S. government web site offers many different kinds of maps of the United States, such as maps that show different types of land, weather, and the number of people living in an area. Explore the links here to learn more about maps. You can also try to make a map yourself.

www.nationalgeographic.com/kids-world-atlas/maps.html
This National Geographic page is full of links to information about maps. The resources listed here will help you create your own maps, find maps for school reports, zoom in on different parts of the world, and much more!

Index